Creative
PARTY CAKES
FOR CHILDREN

TO SIMON AND TAMSIN

Creative PARTY CAKES FOR CHILDREN

Angela Brown

Illustrations by Ann Barrett
Photographs by Mark Mason

W. Foulsham & Co. Ltd.
London ● New York ● Toronto ● Cape Town ● Sydney

W. Foulsham & Company Limited
Yeovil Road, Slough, Berkshire, SL1 4JH

ISBN 0–572–01397–3

Printed in Hong Kong

Contents

Introduction

The focus of any children's party is surely the meal. Whatever form this may take, whether lunch or tea, a picnic or a meal out, the other elements of the party are arranged to fit round this. And at the centre of a birthday meal is — the birthday cake. It is the fact of having a birthday cake that marks the meal as a celebration and, moreover, in the choice of cake, makes it special to one child.

I started making novelty cakes for my own children on their birthdays and they still remember the different cakes they have had on each particular birthday. Now they plan ahead, and new and favourite things tend to be translated into cake requests!

Time and again people asking me for cakes say that, with all the other parts of a party to prepare — the games, the presents, the food — they want to be sure that the cake is going to be successful — something to be remembered. The purpose of this book is to answer both these needs.

It is primarily a book of ideas — not a cookery book. All the cakes are made from a basic Victoria sponge recipe — with the exception of one, the train cake, where the recipe used for the tunnel is a light fatless sponge as in a Swiss roll. The book aims to show in a clear step-by-step sequence how to make each cake.

None of the cakes is difficult to make. Anyone who can make a basic sponge and with a reasonable degree of dexterity — plus a little patience — can make any of the cakes in this book. In fact, making the cakes can be as much fun as the finished result.

In the General Notes and Recipe sections which follow, the two sponge recipes used in the book and the three icing recipes are given along with notes on the preparations of tins, cooling and cutting cakes, the use of food colourings, the use and application of fondant, and other points that may be useful. It is recommended that you read through these sections before starting on any of the cakes.

General Notes

CANDLES

Although only certain of the cakes illustrate the use of candles, these may, of course, be wanted on any cake. Of the cakes where they are not specified, they might best be placed on the board, into piped butter icing rosettes in the Rapunzel, Robot, Pony, Rabbit and Dragon cakes. Use a number 8 nozzle to pipe the rosettes and green or pale pink icing (Rapunzel), ice blue icing (Robot), green or deep pink icing (Pony), pink icing (Rabbit) and yellow icing (Dragon). With the Galleon they could be placed around the ship in the sea. In the Sleeping Beauty cake, leave small spaces between the sections of brambles and put the candles in these, directly into the butter icing. These look very effective when lit.

COLOURINGS

Two kinds of food colouring are used in the cakes. These are liquid colours which are bought in bottles, and concentrated colour which is supplied in tubs and which can be bought in some delicatessens and specialist kitchen shops. These are referred to in the recipes as 'colour' for liquid colour, and 'con. colour' for concentrated colour. The exceptions to this are gold and silver colour which comes in powdered form and should be mixed with a little oil before painting on.

The colours of the concentrated colour tend to be very vivid and pure, which is marvellous where a strong colour is needed. Where a pale result is wanted and concentrated colour is specified, be sure to add only a very little at a time until the colour you need is reached. A good example of this is in the use of Paprika concentrated colour. To make a skin tone only the merest hint is needed. Used more liberally, however, it produces a fine, deep orange as in Rapunzel's prince's clothes and on the Galleon. Where colour is painted on, a fine soft brush should be used. For painting on eyes and mouths use a brush with a very fine tip.

FONDANT ICING

There are on the market very good ready-to-use fondant icings, and using these may well be considered the simpler and quicker procedure. If you prefer to make your own fondant, however, a recipe is given in the Recipe section. Whichever is preferred, its use and application are the same.

COLOURING FONDANT

When adding colour to fondant or marzipan be sure to mix thoroughly, initially with a wooden spoon and then kneading until the colour is thoroughly incorporated.

ROLLING OUT FONDANT

It will be seen that the instructions in the recipes require simply that the fondant (or marzipan in the case of the Pig) is rolled out. A sufficient thickness in almost all cases would be just less than 6mm/¼ inch. Where the requirement differs as, for example, in the crenellations on Rapunzel's tower and on the train, this is specified in the instructions. When rolling both fondant and marzipan, dust the work surface and rolling pin with icing sugar to prevent sticking, and continue to do so as necessary while you work.

HARDENING FONDANT

It is sometimes recommended that sections of fondant are left to harden completely before assembling or placing in position. This can lead to cracking, however, and I prefer to use the fondant while still pliable. There are some instances where a certain degree of drying is required and, again, these are specified in the instructions; for example, the Sleeping Beauty figure. Where this is the case the piece in question should be left for an hour or two, depending on the thickness, and then handled when still slightly pliable so that any tiny cracks can be smoothed over. Modelled pieces of fondant should be placed on to non-stick paper which has been dusted lightly with icing sugar, whether they are to be left to harden or are simply being assembled before being used.

APPLYING FONDANT

Small pieces of fondant can be picked up as they are and applied as specified in the instructions. Large pieces, however, are heavy, and to avoid them stretching out of shape they should be eased over a rolling pin and lifted with the rolling pin taking some of the weight. Care should be taken not to stretch the fondant as it is applied. The area of cake to be covered should first be brushed with sieved apricot jam, using a pastry brush. The fondant will then adhere easily. Where a fondant piece is applied to a fondant surface, egg white, beaten lightly with a fork to break up the albumen, should be used as it will not show.

PREPARATION OF TINS, COOLING AND CUTTING

All the tins need to be greased before use. If the sandwich tins used are the kind with a bar that turns around the base, then these need only be greased. Otherwise they need to be lined with greased greaseproof paper as described below. All other tins and containers, including food tins, loaf tins and basins, need to be lined in this way. First cut pieces of greaseproof paper to fit the container. Lightly grease the container and line with paper, then grease the paper.

When the cake is baked, leave for a few minutes before turning on to a wire rack to cool. This is especially important where the cake is a large one. Peel the paper off while the cake is still warm.

All trimming and cutting is done when the cakes are quite cool, otherwise a clean line will not be achieved. Use a serrated knife as this will give the cleanest edge.

The Recipes

SPONGES

This basic recipe can be varied by adding finely grated orange or lemon rind or flavouring essences. The quantities given here are for a 6-egg mixture. Whatever the quantity given for a particular cake, however, the proportions remain the same. Thus a 5-egg mixture would use 275 g/10 oz each of sugar, fat and flour, an 8-egg mixture would use 450 g/1 lb each.

Victoria Sponge

	Metric	Imperial	American
Margarine or butter	350 g	12 oz	1½ cups
Castor sugar	350 g	12 oz	1½ cups
Eggs	6	6	6
Self-raising flour	350 g	12 oz	3 cups
Baking powder	1 tsp	1 tsp	1 tsp
Milk			

Cream the fat and sugar until light. Sift the flour and baking powder together. Whisk the eggs and add alternately to the creamed ingredients with the sifted flour, beating well after each addition. Add milk as necessary to give a dropping consistency. Bake at 190°C/375°F/Mark 5 until the cake is springy to the touch (test the centre) and has started to shrink from the sides of the tin. With a large cake be sure to leave it long enough for the centre to be cooked.

Light Fatless Sponge

	Metric	Imperial	American
Eggs	6	6	6
Castor sugar	225 g	8 oz	1 cup
Plain flour	225 g	8 oz	2 cups
Hot water	30 ml	2 tbsp	2 tbsp

Sift the flour. Whisk the eggs and sugar in a bowl over a pan of hot water until light and creamy. The mixture should be quite thick. Remove the bowl from the heat and whisk until cool. Fold in half the sifted flour using a metal spoon. Fold in the remaining flour in the same way and add the hot water, stirring lightly. Pour the mixture into the prepared tin (see General Notes) and tip the tin to allow the mixture to cover the surface. Bake at 220°C/425°F/ Mark 7 for about 10–15 minutes until risen and golden brown. Turn out onto wire rack to cool.

ICINGS

Fondant Icing

	Metric	Imperial	American
Egg white	1	1	1
Icing sugar	450 g	1 lb	3 cups
Liquid glucose	30 ml	2 tbsp	2 tbsp

Add the sieved icing sugar and the warmed liquid glucose to the egg white gradually, until the required consistency is obtained. The fondant should be pliable but firm. If it is too stiff add more egg white; if it is not stiff enough, add more icing sugar. When not being used, fondant should be wrapped in cling film and stored in an airtight container at room temperature. Do not keep it in the refrigerator.

Glacé Icing

This is made by adding warm water to sifted icing sugar until the required consistency is reached. The icing should be at least thick enough to coat the back of a spoon. Add the water very gradually as very little is needed. 50–75 g/2–3 oz icing sugar will need only 7–15 ml/½–1 tbsp water.

Butter Icing

This is made by adding sifted icing sugar gradually to creamed butter or margarine, moistening with milk to give a good spreading consistency. The quantities given in the instructions refer to the amount of fat used, with 1½–2 times this weight being added in icing sugar. Thus a quantity given as 225 g/8 oz butter icing requires 225 g/8 oz butter or margarine and 350–450 g/12 oz–1 lb icing sugar. If liquid colour is to be used and the colour needed is a strong one, take account of this when making up the butter icing and make it a little stiffer than otherwise. More milk can always be added after the desired colour has been achieved.

It is a good idea to secure all the cakes to the boards with butter icing. This will keep them firmly to the board while being worked on and in the case of a tall cake without any other support, such as Rapunzel's tower, will ensure that it cannot topple over.

Merry-Go-Round

INGREDIENTS
1.6 kg/1 lb 12 oz butter icing
Christmas red con. colour
Ice blue con. colour
Green colour
4 plain wafers
8 fan wafers
Mimosa balls
Liquorice Allsorts

EQUIPMENT
Nos. 3 and 8 nozzles
Piping bag
25 cm/10 in octagonal tin
25 cm/10 in round board
23 cm/9 in round thin board
9 striped pencils
8 merry-go-round figures

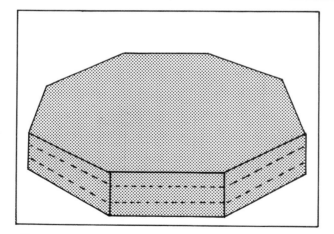

1 Bake a 7-egg sponge mixture in the octagonal tin. Cut cool cake into three horizontally. Colour approximately 450 g/1 lb butter icing red, 225 g/8 oz green and 100 g/4 oz blue.

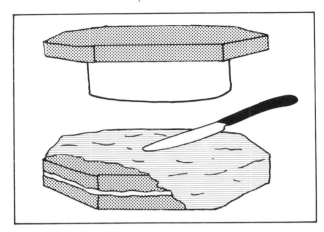

2 Put the top layer on to thin board for roundabout top, and place on a cake tin so that sides are free to decorate. Sandwiching together with red butter icing, place remaining two layers on 25 cm/10 in board. Cover base and top entirely with red butter icing, smoothing all surfaces.

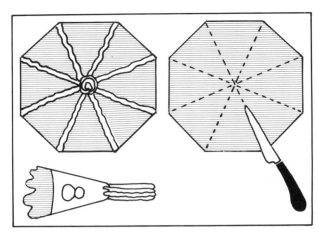

3 Working on the base only and using no. 8 nozzle pipe green butter icing from the centre to each point, dividing the top surface into 8 sections. Pipe a rosette in the centre. Mark the same lines lightly with a knife on roundabout top as a guide for later piping.

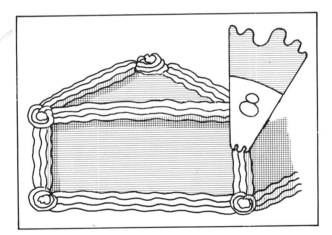

4 Using no. 8 nozzle pipe green icing around the edge of each outer panel of the base. Pipe a rosette at each corner and place a mimosa ball in each.

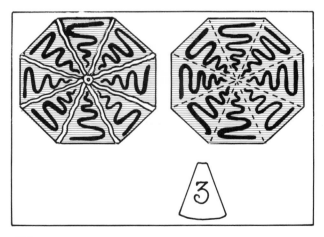

5 Using no. 3 nozzle and blue icing pipe a wavy line in each segment on the upper surface of the base and in each marked segment of the top. If candles are to be used they can be put in roundabout top at this stage.

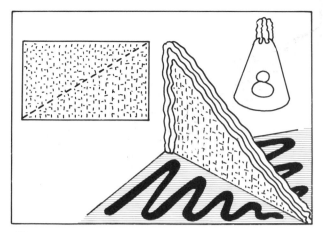

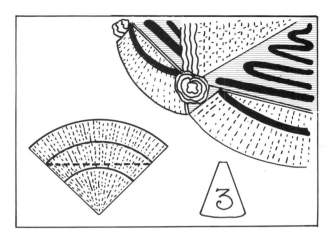

6 Cut the four plain wafers diagonally and place on edge, narrow end to centre, along each of marked lines on roundabout top. Using no. 8 nozzle and green icing carefully pipe along edge of each wafer. Pipe a large rosette in the centre of roundabout top and decorate with mimosa ball.

7 Cut across fan wafers about 2.5 cm/1 in from the point by making a perforated line with the tip of a sharp knife. Using butter icing to secure, press a cut wafer firmly but gently to each side section of roundabout top to give a scalloped effect. Using no. 3 nozzle and blue icing pipe a loop on each wafer. Using no. 8 nozzle and green icing pipe round cake along upper edge of fan wafers.

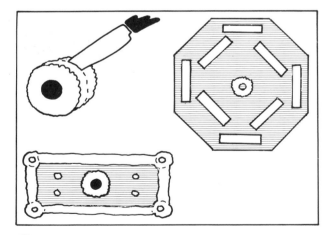

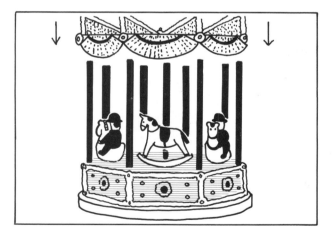

8 Cut four yellow liquorice allsorts in half horizontally and place in the centre of each side panel of base. Cut a fifth one in same way and remove liquorice centre from one half. Place yellow ring in centre rosette. Finish decorations with mimosa balls or halved blue allsorts. Place merry-go-round figures in each section, alternately nearer centre and edge.

9 Making sure you keep them vertical, press pencils into base of merry-go-round, one in the centre and one about 12 mm½ in from each angle. Press them in until they touch the board. If there is a rounded end to the pencils put it downward so that the flat ends are ready to support the top. Carefully lift the top from underneath and place centrally on to pencils.

Robot

INGREDIENTS

1.5 kg/3 lb 4 oz fondant
50 g/2 oz butter icing
300 g/10 oz glacé icing
Ice blue cor. colour
Silver lustre colour
Silver balls
Jelly sweets
Sieved apricot jam
Egg white

EQUIPMENT

Nos. 2 and 8 nozzles
Piping bag
Fine paintbrush
900 ml/2 pint basin
Four 23 cm/7 in round
sandwich tins
15 × 7 cm/6 × 3 in
rectangular tin
Pastry brush

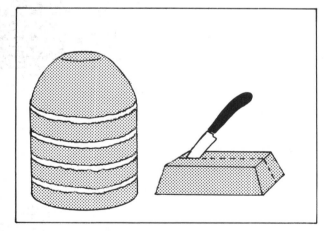

1 Bake a 12-egg sponge mixture in the sandwich tins, basin and loaf tin, filling the latter only half full. Trim all tops flat. Sandwiching together with butter icing, layer round sponges in centre of board, with upturned basin cake on top. Cut loaf cake in half lengthwise.

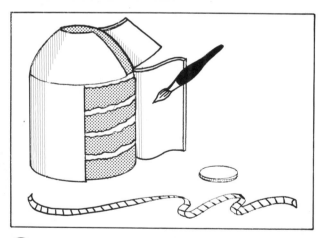

2 Roll out 1 kg/2 lb white fondant. Measure height and circumference of cake and cut a rectangle to fit the round cakes, a curved strip for the dome and a circle for the top. Brush cake with jam and apply, using a rolling pin to lift fondant.

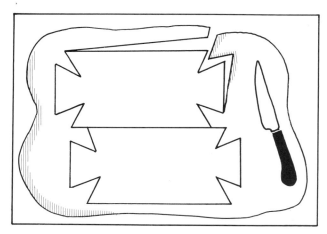

3 Roll 225 g/8 oz white fondant and cut shapes to cover the two oblong pieces as illustrated. Brush these with jam and apply fondant.

4 Place oblongs on board at each side of robot body. Roll 100 g/4 oz white fondant about 2.5 cm/1 in thick and cut two pieces 4 cm/1½ in wide and 10 cm/4 in long. Slightly flatten and round one end and make patterns with the handle of a teaspoon and the flat blade of a knife. Attach to robot with egg white, rounded end at the top.

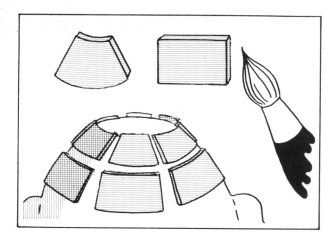

5 Colour 225 g/8 oz fondant blue and roll out. Cut twelve shapes for top of robot as illustrated, six of each kind. Cut two strips to go round robot, 2.5 cm/1 in wide and 1 cm/½ in wide, squares for the ends of feet and arch shapes to fit into recesses on legs. Attach with egg white.

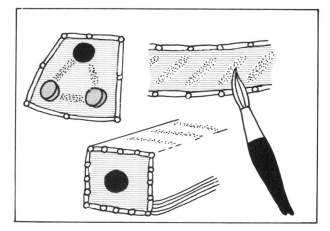

6 With glacé icing and no. 2 nozzle pipe round all blue shapes. Place silver balls in piping round all pieces. Attach jelly lights to top pieces with egg white. Mix silver colouring into a paste with a little oil and paint lines on top panels, lower band and top of feet. Using no. 8 nozzle and 50 g/2 oz blue butter icing pipe rosettes along base of robot and a line along base of feet.

Rapunzel

INGREDIENTS
900 g/2 lb fondant
75–125 g/3– 4 oz butter icing
125 g/4 oz desiccated coconut
Chocolate brown colour
Green colour
Paprika con. colour
Christmas red con. colour
Egg yellow con. colour
Sieved apricot jam
Egg white

EQUIPMENT
No. 2 nozzle
Piping bag
Pastry brush
One 10 × 11 cm/ 4 × 4 ½ in food tin
Two 8 × 10 cm/3 × 4 in food tins
28 cm/11 in round board
Fine paintbrush
Non-stick paper

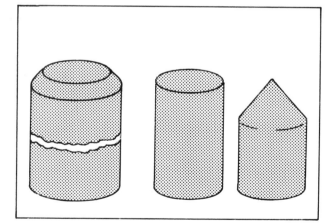

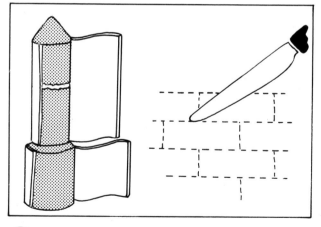

1 Bake a 5-egg sponge mixture in the 3 tins. Trim the tops of large and one small cake flat. Cut top edge of large cake and second small cake as illustrated. The large cake can be cut and sandwiched with butter icing. Position large cake slightly off centre of board. Place untrimmed small cake on this and pointed cake on top, sandwiching with butter icing.

2 Colour 700 g/1½ lb fondant light brown. Measure height and circumference of cakes, roll fondant and cut to fit straight sides of tower. Brush cakes with jam and apply fondant. Score lines with the tip of a sharp knife for stones, marking horizontal lines first, then vertical.

3 Cut arched recess about 2.5 cm/1 in deep in top cake for window. Colour 25 g/1 oz fondant dark grey and use to cover inside of window. Colour remaining brown fondant a slightly darker brown. Roll out a small quantity and cut pieces to trim window as illustrated, securing with egg white.

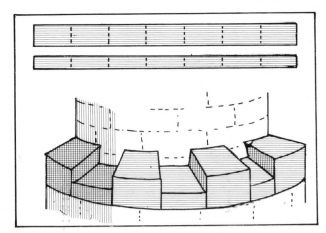

4 Roll a small quantity of dark brown fondant to 6 mm/¼ in thick and a similar quantity to 12 mm/½ in thick. Using jam to secure, place round ledge on lower section of tower to form crenellations.

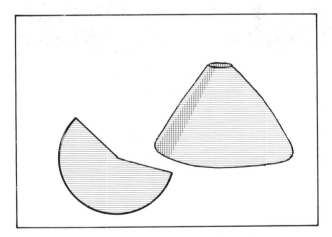

5 From thin card, cut a circle 13 cm/5 in in diameter. Cut a line to centre and fold into a cone. Check that it fits top of cake – it should overlap slightly – and staple to secure. Roll remaining brown fondant and cut a circle the same size as card, cutting out a wedge as shown. Fold fondant shape round card, securing join with egg white.

6 Press the end of a teaspoon into roof all round, working up from the bottom. Make a roll of fondant and pinch into pinnacle shape as shown. Press lines in this with the blunt side of a knife. Attach to roof with egg white and leave to harden slightly. Spread butter icing on angled top of cake, remove card cone and position roof.

7 Make Rapunzel from about 75 g/3 oz fondant as shown, using egg white to join pieces together. Colour small quantities of fondant flesh, deep pink and yellow for the head and arm, body and sleeve, and hair respectively. Paint blue dots for eyes and a red dot for a mouth.

8 Place Rapunzel in position in window before applying hair, securing her with egg white. Roll three lengths of yellow fondant, press one end of each together and plait. Press at other end to join and score end with a sharp knife. Attach to side of Rapunzel's head, securing there and down the length of tower with egg white. Press a little yellow fondant through a sieve and attach to head for remaining hair.

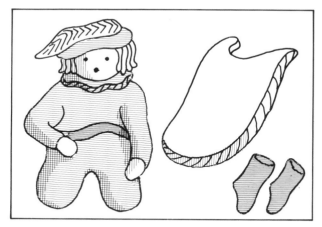

9 Make prince from about 125 g/4 oz fondant, using flesh for head and hands; deep orange (use paprika) for body, legs and hat; brown for boots and belt and yellow for feather and cloak. Press the edge of a teaspoon round cloak to finish. Pipe hair with no. 2 nozzle and brown butter icing. Paint blue dots for eyes and a paprika dot for mouth.

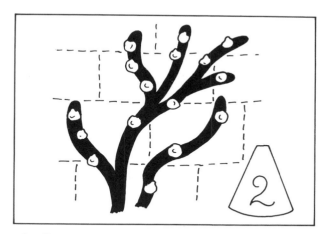

10 Using no. 2 nozzle and green butter icing, pipe stems up tower. With same nozzle and pink butter icing, pipe dots for flowers. Cover board with green butter icing and cover this with desiccated coconut coloured green.

21

Easter Rabbit

INGREDIENTS
375 g/13 oz fondant
225 g/8 oz butter icing
50 g/2 oz shredded coconut
Green colour
Brown colour
Pink colour
Egg white
Chocolate eggs

EQUIPMENT
Two 900 g/2 lb loaf tins
Fine paint brush
Small basket
Whiskers (as for soft toy
making)
30 cm/12 in round board

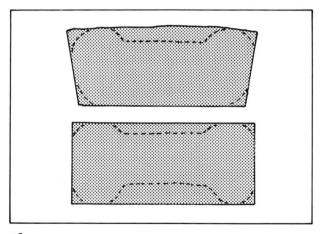

1 Bake a 7-egg sponge mixture in two 900 g/2 lb tins. With one loaf cake, cut haunches as shown, rounding all edges.

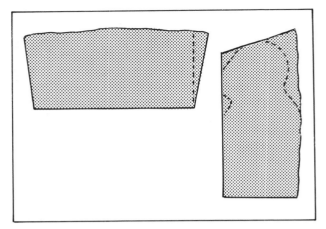

2 Trim one end of the second loaf cake vertically. Stand the cake on this end and cut the body and head as illustrated, shaping the back of the head and rounding all edges.

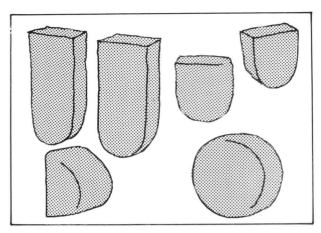

3 From the trimmings cut two front legs, two hind feet, a nose and a round tail.

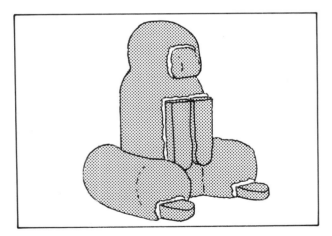

4 Colour 225 g/8 oz butter icing light brown. Use it to secure the pieces in place and then cover rabbit entirely with butter icing. Apply butter icing thinly under coat area and roughen remaining surface with a knife. Cover board with butter icing and cover with 50 g/2 oz coconut coloured green.

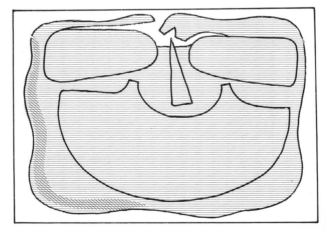

5 Colour 225 g/8 oz fondant bright green. Roll out to about 6 mm/¼ in thick and cut body and sleeves of coat as shown.

6 Brush area to be covered by coat with egg white and ease main coat piece into position; joining tabs at front of neck and lifting lower edge at the sides. Place front wedge section between arms and finally apply sleeves pressing edges gently to join. Decorate shoulder edges of sleeves with the tip of a sharp knife.

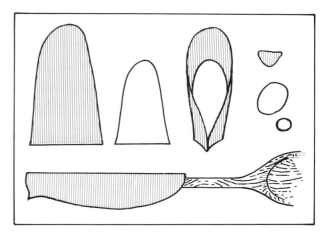

7 Colour 50 g/2 oz fondant mid-brown and 25 g/1 oz light brown. Roll darker fondant 6 mm/¼ in thick and cut ears. Roll lighter fondant more thinly and cut ear linings and features. Using egg white to secure, assemble eyes and ears, then fold the sides of ears to the centre at the base. Lay ears over the handles of two wooden spoons to curve. Leave to harden. Roll 15 tiny balls of light fondant for flower centres.

8 Colour 50 g/2 oz fondant bright pink. Roll 5 balls 12 mm/½ in in diameter and one ball 2.5 cm/1 in. Flatten small balls and pull in edges in five places. Make small holes in centres with a sharp point and secure three tiny balls with egg white. Press large ball into a rectangle about 3 cm/1½ in long. Pull in the centre and incise lines. Secure a scrap of flat pink fondant across the centre. Leave to harden.

9 Cut holes in top of head and set in ears, covering join with fresh butter cream. Secure features with butter cream and bow with egg white. Press in whiskers making holes with a pin. Place basket and eggs on grass and intersperse with flowers. Using a fine brush and brown colouring highlight centres of eyes, edges of ears and eyes, peaks of fur and centres of flowers.

Steam Engine

INGREDIENTS

700 g/1 lb 8 oz fondant
250 g/9 oz butter icing
225 g/8 oz shredded coconut
50 g/2 oz desiccated coconut
Green colour
Black colour
Blue colour
Christmas red con. colour
1 White marshmallow
2 miniature Liquorice Allsorts
(1 black, 1 yellow)
Apricot jam
Egg white

EQUIPMENT

No. 2 nozzle
Piping bag
Round cocktail cutter
25 cm/10 in ring tin
35 cm/14 in round board
Candles and holders
Non-stick paper

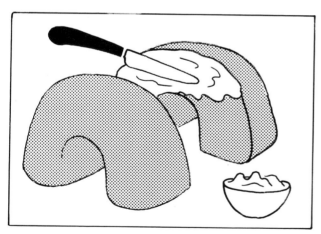

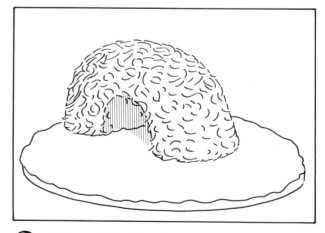

1 Bake a 6-egg fatless sponge mixture in ring tin. Trim the top of cake flat and cut cake in half crosswise. Sandwiching halves together with butter icing, position on board as a archway slightly to one side, securing to board with butter icing.

2 Colour 225 g/8 oz butter icing and 225 g/8 oz shredded coconut green. Cover arch and board with butter icing. Sprinkle arch with shredded coconut.

3 Colour 125 g/4 oz fondant brown and roll out. Cut 20 sleepers 6 mm × 4 cm/1¾ × ½ in and lay round board from one side of archway to the other. Toast 50 g/2 oz desiccated coconut, and when cool sprinkle between sleepers. Cover rest of board with green shredded coconut.

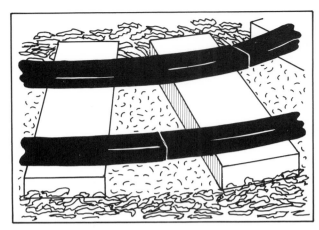

4 Colour 75 g/3 oz fondant black. Roll out and cut strips 6 mm/¼ in wide and lay over sleepers as rails.

5 Colour 75 g/3 oz fondant grey and roll out. Cut 18 wheels with round cocktail cutter. With the tip of a knife score spokes.

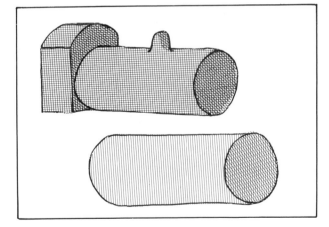

6 Colour 225 g/8 oz fondant, or marzipan if preferred, red and 175 g/6 oz blue. Make two red rolls for carriages, flattening each end. Use 125 g/4 oz blue to make a similar roll for engine. With remaining blue make a whistle for engine and a slab, about 12 mm/½ in thick, 12 mm/½ in wider and 2 cm/¾ in taller than roll. Leave to harden then join with egg white.

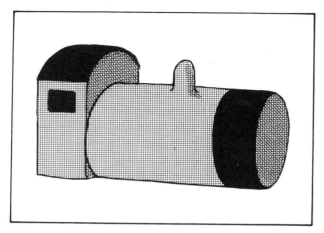

7 Roll remaining black fondant thinly and cut strips for front end of engine and the roof of the cabin and two rectangles for windows. Apply with egg white.

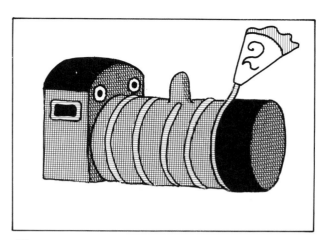

8 Using no. 2 nozzle and red butter icing pipe round windows and five lines around engine as illustrated. Secure with egg white a black liquorice allsort to engine for funnel. Cut slices from a yellow liquorice allsort and apply to front of cabin.

9 Fix three wheels to each side of engine and carriages. Cut 6 mm/¼ in wide strips from thinly rolled black fondant and secure across wheels with egg white. Pull a white marshmallow to break the skin. Attach one end to funnel with a little jam. Be sure to pull marshmallow enough, otherwise it will tend to contract, and do this just before cake is needed.

10 Colour a scrap of fondant grey. Roll thickly and model features of face as shown. Cut a round shape the same size as end of engine and enclosing modelled face. Make eyes from scraps of white and black fondant. Secure in place with egg white. Leave to harden, then secure to train.

Fire-Breathing dragon

INGREDIENTS
975 g/2 lb 3 oz fondant
75 g/3 oz butter icing
Green colour
Egg yellow con colour
Grape violet con colour
Black colour
15 g/½ oz Sugar (granulated or castor)
Sieved apricot jam
Egg white

EQUIPMENT
Nos. 2, 3 and 8 nozzles
Piping bag
Pastry brush
20 cm/8in round sandwich tin
900 g/2 lb loaf tin
35 cm/14in round board
Non-stick paper

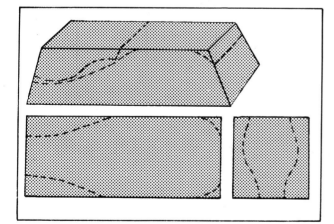

1 Bake a 6-egg sponge mixture in the loaf tin and sandwich tin. Trim loaf cake flat and turn over. Cut loaf cake horizontally as shown to give outline of body. Then make vertical cuts on body section, rounding back end. Cut head from remaining section as illustrated.

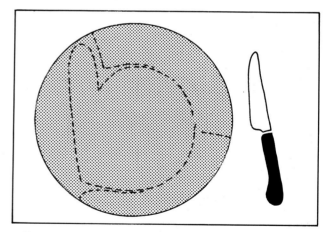

2 From round cake cut two tail sections and back haunches and feet as illustrated. Cut back haunches section in half horizontally to make two.

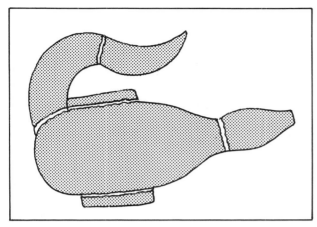

3 Assemble dragon on board, positioning body to one side to allow room for tail and joining pieces with butter icing. Turn the end section of tail over so that the tail curves as an 'S' shape.

4 Colour 700 g/1½ lb fondant green. Roll out and cut shapes for head and haunches as shown. Score all over with lines using a knife. Brush cake with jam and apply. Cut two small triangles for ears and position on head, securing with egg white.

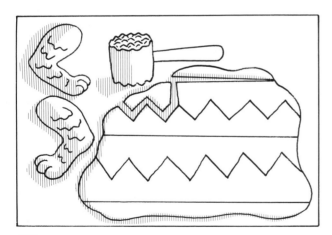

5 Cut strips of scales from remaining rolled fondant. If wished, a meat tenderiser can be used to texture the surface before cutting the scales. Use trimmings of green fondant to roll and shape two forelegs as shown, scoring surface with a knife.

6 Brush tail and uncovered area of body with jam and cover with scales starting at end of tail and working towards head, overlapping layers slightly. Using the handle of a teaspoon, pull fondant into folds above and below eye area.

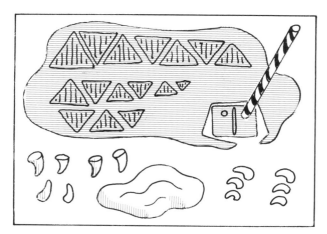

7 Colour 50 g/2 oz fondant purple and roll out. Cut about 16 spines grading from 12 mm/½ in to 3 cm/1¼ in high. Score with vertical lines. Cut snout from purple fondant and make two holes with the end of a straw. With the back of a knife make an indented line down the centre to take the 'fire'. Make six teeth about 12 mm/½ in long and six claws from scraps of white fondant.

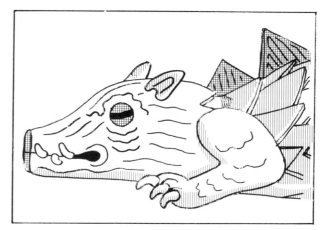

8 Attach spines with egg white along back and tail placing largest in the centre of back and the smaller each side, ending with the smallest towards the tip of the tail. Colour a scrap of fondant yellow and make flat round eyes, indenting a line across centre. Fix a thin roll of purple fondant in this line. Position eyes, teeth and claws as illustrated, securing all features with egg white.

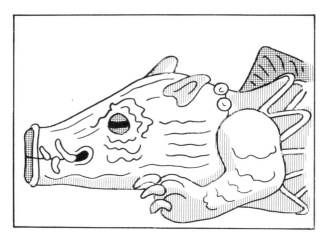

9 Colour 75 g/3 oz butter icing yellow and using no. 3 nozzle pipe dots along join of scales to head and along top of haunches. Using no. 2 nozzle, outline scales with yellow and pipe line where snout joins head.

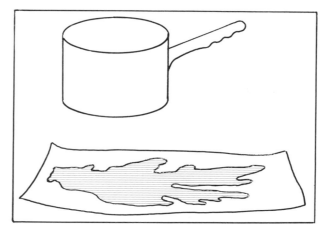

10 Colour 125 g/4 oz fondant dark grey and 125 g/4 oz light grey. Chop when beginning to dry. Brush board with jam and cover with 'stones'. Dissolve 15 g/½ oz sugar in 1 tablespoon water and boil without stirring until a caramel colour. Pour spoonfuls into long shapes on non-stick paper and allow to set. Use the best shape as 'flames' from dragon's mouth.

Galleon

INGREDIENTS

1.1 kg/2 lb 8 oz butter icing
25 g/1 oz fondant
75 g/3 oz plain or milk chocolate
Paprika con. colour
Egg yellow con. colour
Green colour
Holly green con. colour
Blue colour
Long matchmakers
3 pieces rice paper

EQUIPMENT

3 garden sticks
Red and yellow paper
Paste
Nos. 2, 3 and 8 nozzles
Piping bag
Two 900 g/2 lb loaf tins
35 cm/14 in square board

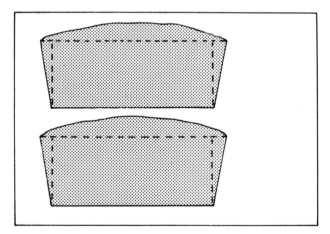

1 Bake an 8-egg sponge mixture in the two loaf tins. Trim the tops flat and the ends square.

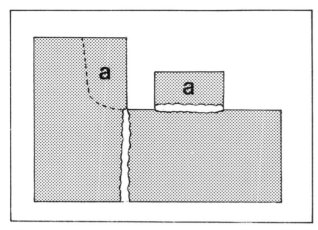

2 Place one cake lengthwise diagonally on board and one upright as shown. Cut out piece 'a' from upright cake and place it across flat cake as illustrated. Sandwich all pieces together with butter icing.

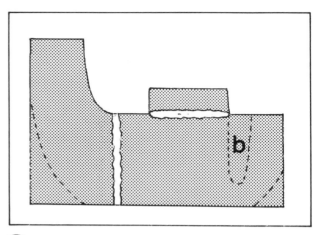

3 Cut out piece 'b' from flat cake and set aside. Cut a curved slice from each end of cake to round the undersides as illustrated.

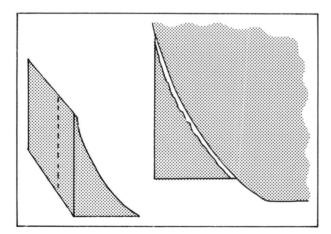

4 Cut a 12 mm/½ in piece off each of these curved pieces and replace under each end of cake as supports.

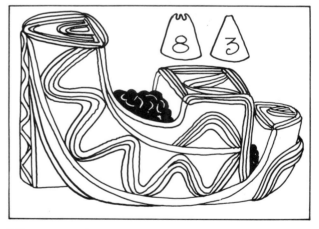

5 Colour 450 g/1 lb butter icing deep orange and cover ship entirely, smoothing surface. Grate 75 g/3 oz chocolate and place on the two recessed surfaces. Colour 175 g/6 oz butter icing yellow and, using no. 3 nozzle for plain lines and no. 8 nozzle for zigzags, pipe lines as in illustration. Pipe dots on inside (front) surface of both tall sections with no. 3 nozzle.

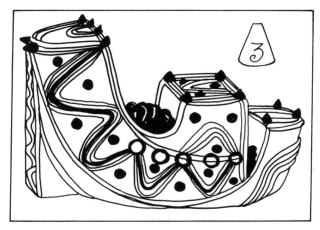

6 Colour 50 g/2 oz butter icing green and using no. 2 nozzle pipe a thin line on top of all zigzag lines, if wished, and five circles on each side of galleon to mark the positions of oars. Pipe dots as illustrated with no. 3 nozzle.

7 Colour remaining 450 g/1 lb butter icing blue-green (using holly green con. colour and blue colour), and using no. 12 nozzle pipe sea all over board making waves as you do so. Put Matchmakers for oars in position, putting one end in each green circle and lowering into the sea. Press one Matchmaker into bow for bowsprit.

8 Model two fish from a little white fondant, omitting tails. Incise a line for mouth with a knife and use the tip of a sharp knife to press scales. Make holes for eyes. Mix silver food colouring to a paste with a little oil and paint fish. Position in sea.

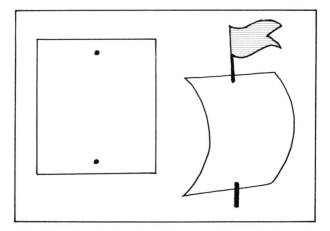

9 Cut one stick to 43 cm/17 in and two to 30 cm/12 in. Cut one red flag and two yellow. Paste straight end of each flag and stick round one end of each mast. Cut one piece of rice paper 18 × 14 cm/7½ × 5½ in and two pieces 16 × 14 cm/6½ × 5½ in. Make two holes in each with a skewer for masts. Pull up sail to billow. Press masts into galleon down to board.

Pony

INGREDIENTS
575 g/1 lb 4 oz butter icing
50 g/2 oz fondant
Grape violet con. colour
Pink colour
Green colour
Liquorice Allsort
Egg white

EQUIPMENT
No. 8 nozzle
Piping bag
900 g/2 lb loaf tin
450 g/1 lb loaf tin
25 cm/10 in round board

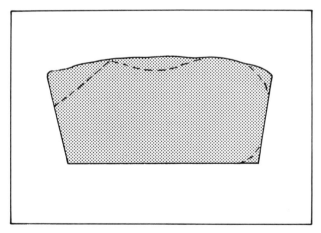

1 Bake a 6-egg sponge mixture in the two loaf tins. From larger cake cut shape for main body as illustrated, making horizontal cut first, then vertical.

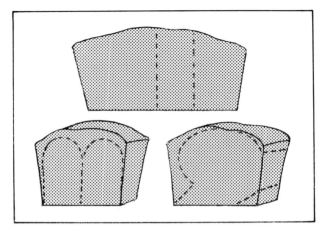

2 Cut small cake in half across its width. Cut one section in half again. From one quarter section cut one hind leg and from the other cut two forelegs as illustrated.

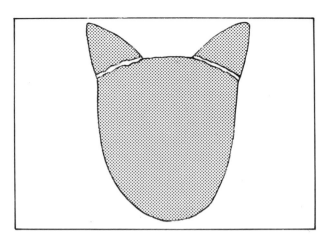

3 From the remaining half of the small block cut the head and ears as illustrated, making vertical cut for head first, then horizontal.

4 Assemble pony on board joining all pieces with butter icing. Cut the second hind leg from a left-over piece of sponge and place in position. Colour 350 g/12 oz butter icing pale mauve and cover cake entirely, smoothing surface.

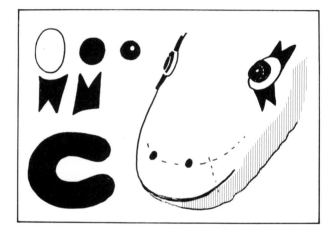

5 Incise mouth with a knife and nostrils with the end of a skewer. Make the eyes. Cut two circles and four shapes from a black round liquorice allsort as shown. Make two circles from purple fondant and two small dots of white fondant. Join pieces together with egg white and press into position on pony. Make horseshoe from purple fondant and position on tucked under back leg as shown.

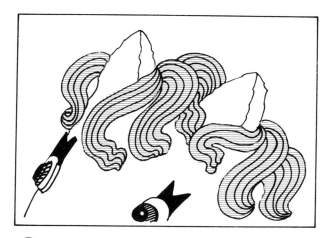

6 Colour 50 g/2 oz butter icing green. Spread on board and cover with 125 g/4 oz shredded coconut coloured green. Colour 175 g/6 oz butter icing pink and using no. 8 nozzle pipe a flowing mane and tail.

7 From 25-50 g/ 1-2 oz white fondant make flowers. Roll into a ball and press to flatten. Pull in edges with the back of a knife to make petals. Attach three tiny yellow fondant balls to centre of flowers with egg white. Place flowers in position on pony and in mane and tail.

Sleeping Beauty

INGREDIENTS
1.1 kg/2 lb 5 oz fondant
75-100 g/3-4 oz butter icing
25 g/1 oz glacé icing
Grape violet con. colour
Paprika con. colour
Egg yellow con. colour
Green colour
Gold lustre colour
Silver balls
Two pieces rice paper
Sieved apricot jam
Egg white

EQUIPMENT
Nos. 2 and 8 nozzles
Piping bag
Fine paintbrush
Pastry brush
Two 18 cm/7 in square
sandwich tins
Two 62 cm/25 in lengths of wire
2 garden sticks
Pliers
Paste
30 cm/12 in round board
Non-stick paper

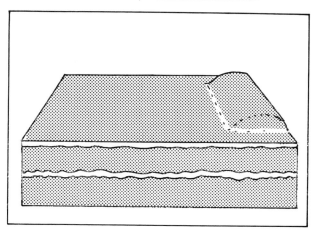

1 Bake a 5-egg sponge mixture in the square tins. Trim tops flat and sandwich together with butter icing. Place in centre of board. Use trimmings to build up pillow as shown, securing with butter icing.

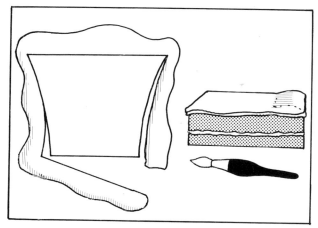

2 Colour 1 kg/2 lb fondant pale pink and roll out sufficient to cut a piece the same size as top of cake, allowing for mound of pillow as shown. Brush cake with jam and apply fondant, pressing gently around edges of pillow.

3 Roll about 500 g/ 1 lb fondant and cut strips as deep as cake. Brush sides of cake with jam and edge of fondant on bed with egg white and apply strip, making folds as you do so to form frill. Roll small quantity of fondant slightly thinner and cut 12 mm½ inch strips. Apply round pillow in same way, attaching with egg white.

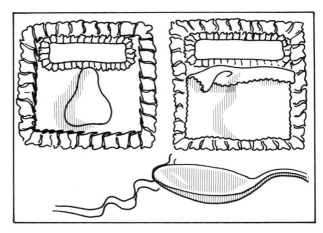

4 Shape about 50 g/2 oz white fondant to make shape of skirt and lay on bed. Roll remaining pink fondant. Cut a square 2.5 cm/ 1 in larger than cake and press a teaspoon round edge to finish. Fold back one end. Using a rolling pin lay over bed starting at bottom end. Lift one side of folded edge. Lift centre to take body.

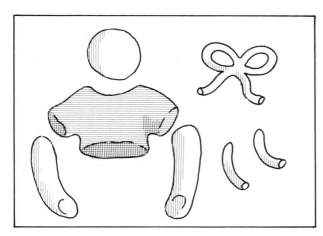

5 Colour small quantities fondant flesh and purple. Model Sleeping Beauty's head and arms from flesh coloured fondant and body and sleeves from purple. Join pieces with egg white. Make bow from small roll and trim sleeves with narrow strips of white fondant. Place figure on non-stick paper and leave to harden slightly.

6 Place figure in bed so that the arms rest over coverlet. Using no. 2 nozzle and yellow butter icing, pipe hair. Paint blue dots for eyes and a red dot for mouth. Paint purple flowers (dots) and green leaves over coverlet. Make small quantity of quite stiff glacé icing and pipe a dot in centre of each flower, along inner edge of pillow frill and top edge of valance.

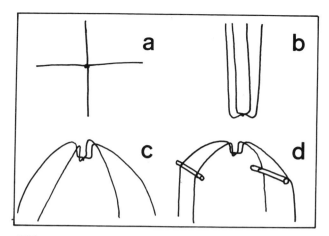

7 Cross the two pieces of wire in centres and twist around each other to hold. Bend wires up 12 mm/½ in from cross and then down 12 mm/½ in from first bend. You now have a recess to take the crown. 11 cm/4½ in from second bend wind wire round 16 cm/6½ in stick so that sticks are opposite. Bend down so that structure stands square. Insert into cake, pressing through to board about 12 mm/½ in from corners.

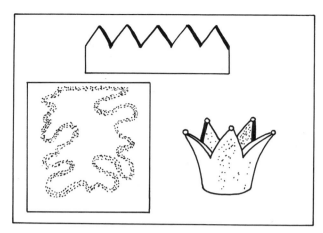

8 Colour 25 g/1 oz fondant yellow and roll out. Cut crown, roll up and secure join with egg white. Fix a silver ball to each point in same way. Cut 2 pieces of rice paper the height of bed posts and width of bed. Mix gold colouring into a paste with a little oil and paint a swirling pattern over paper. Paint crown and wire structure including cross sticks.

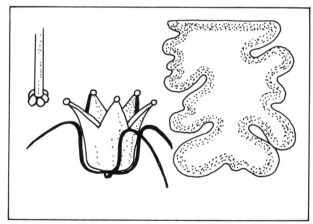

9 Cut round outer edge of pattern on paper. Paste top edge of paper and secure to each cross stick. Pipe dots of glacé icing round wire where it inserts into bed at each corner. Place crown in position.

10 Melt 150 g/ 6 oz chocolate in a double saucepan. Using no. 3 nozzle trail 'brambles' on to non-stick paper about 5-6 cm/2-2½ in deep. Before completely set cut into 7-8 cm/3-4 in sections. Pipe flowers (dots) on, using no. 2 nozzle and pink butter icing. Using no. 8 nozzle pipe rosettes of deeper pink butter icing round board and set brambles in upright.

Space Rocket

INGREDIENTS
1.1 kg/2 lb 8 oz fondant
350 g/12 oz butter icing
Egg yellow con. colour
Chocolate brown colour
Black colour
Green colour
Silver balls
Jelly sweets
1 flat based ice-cream cone
Sieved apricot jam
Egg white

EQUIPMENT
No. 3 nozzle
Piping bag
Two 10 × 11 cm 4 × 4 ½ in
food tins
23 × 18 cm/9 × 7 in
rectangular tin
35 cm/14 in round board
Candles and holders
Toy space figures (optional)
Pastry brush

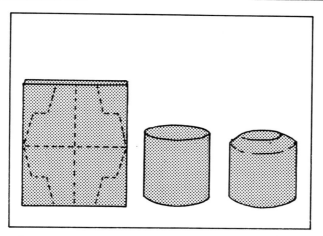

1 Bake a 10-egg sponge mixture in the two food tins and the rectangular tin. Trim the tops flat. Cut the top edge of one food tin cake at an angle. Cut four rocket supports from rectangular cake as illustrated.

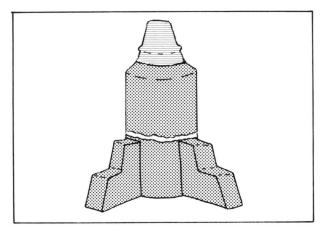

2 Assemble cake in centre of board. Secure supports to rocket with butter icing and place upturned cone on top of cake.

3 Roll 1.1 kg/2 lb 8 oz white fondant and cut out pieces as shown in illustration: four pieces for between supports, eight sides of supports, four strips for outer edges of supports, one rectangle for rocket body, one curved strip for ledge, one wide curved strip for cone, one circle for top of cone.

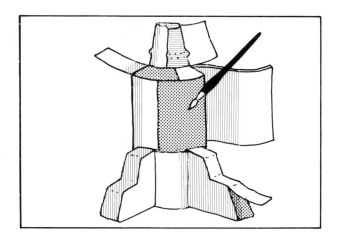

4 Brush cake with jam and apply pieces to cake in this order: a) between supports b) main body c) ledge d) sides of supports e) outer edge of supports. Brush cone with egg white and apply fondant first to sides, pressing gently round ridge and then put circle on top.

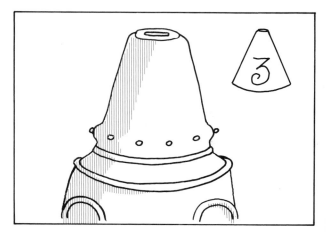

5 Press silver balls round ridge of cone. Colour 100 g/4 oz butter icing yellow ochre, using yellow and brown colouring. Using no. 3 nozzle pipe a line over all joins. Press a round shape (e.g. a cutter) lightly into rocket body above each space between supports (i.e. four circles) and pipe a circle over marking.

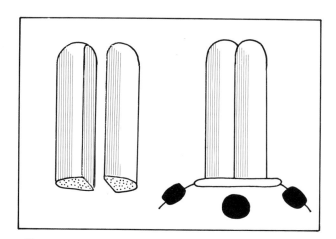

6 Secure jelly lights in position with egg white (as in photograph). Melt a little chocolate in a double saucepan and join two finger biscuits. Cut one end flat and press into top of rocket.

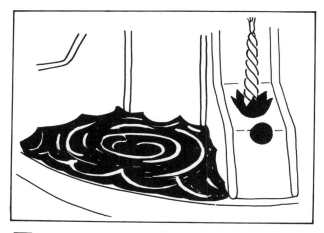

7 Colour 225 g/8 oz butter icing with black and green and spread on board. Roughen surface and make 'craters' with the back of a teaspoon. Place candles on rocket and space figures on moon surface if wished.

Toy Bear

INGREDIENTS
400 g/15 oz butter icing
100 g/4 oz fondant
Egg yellow con. colour
Green colour
Blue colour
Chocolate brown colour
Liquorice Allsort
Egg white

EQUIPMENT
No. 8 nozzle
Piping bag
23 × 18 cm/9 × 7 in
rectangular tin
18 cm/7 in round sandwich tin
23 cm/9 in round board
Candles

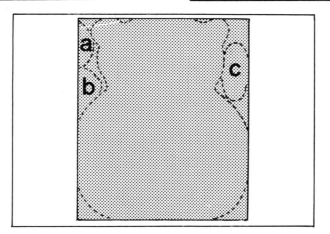

1 Bake a 7-egg sponge mixture in the rectangular and round tins. From rectangle cut out main body shape and pieces for the back of the head (a), nose (b) and cheeks (c).

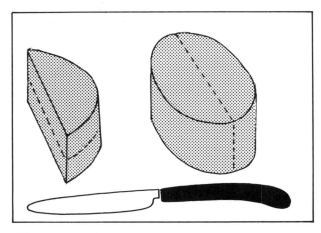

2 Cut piece (a) horizontally to make two pieces for the back of the head and piece (c) vertically to make two cheek pieces.

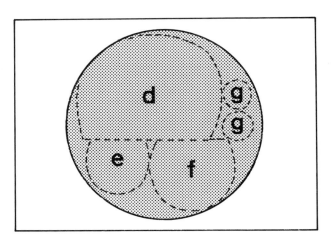

3 Cut the round cake as illustrated. The pieces will be used for the back of the bear (d and e), the tummy (f) and feet (g).

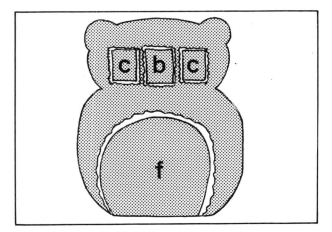

4 Assemble the front of the bear as illustrated while cake is still lying flat. Joining all pieces with butter icing, use piece 'f' on body and pieces 'c' and 'b' on face.

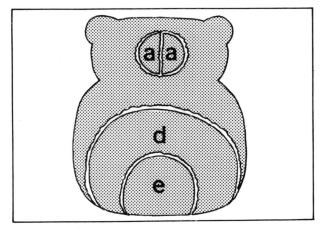

5 Stand bear up and secure to board with butter icing. Assemble back of bear using pieces 'd' and 'e' on body and 'a' on head and joining all pieces with butter icing.

6 Put feet (g) in position and trim edges on cake where necessary to give a rounded effect. Colour 375 g/14 oz butter icing yellow and cover bear entirely, moulding the shape of arms as you do so. Roughen surface all over with a fork.

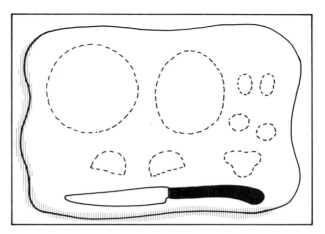

7 Roll 100 g/4 oz white fondant and cut shapes for tummy, face, feet, ears, eyes and nose as illustrated. Position face, ears and feet on bear.

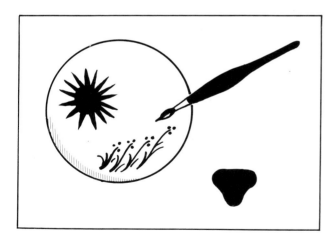

8 Using yellow, green and blue colouring and a fine brush paint picture on fondant tummy. Paint nose piece yellow. Allow to dry. Position on bear, fixing nose to face with egg white. Using no. 8 nozzle and the remaining butter icing coloured blue, pipe rosettes on board for the number of candles required and place a candle in each.

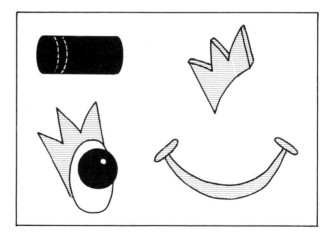

9 Make eyes and mouth. Cut shapes as illustrated and roll a mouth from brown fondant. Cut two slices from a black round liquorice allsort. Assemble eyes as shown, putting a small dot of white fondant on the black. Join all pieces with egg white and secure in position in the same way. (Note: the small bears in the photograph were made from marzipan.)

Father Christmas and his Sleigh

INGREDIENTS
1.5 kg/2 lb 8 oz fondant
75 g/3 oz butter icing
Green colour
Black colour
Chocolate brown colour
Blue colour
Christmas red con. colour.
Paprika con. colour
Egg yellow con. colour
Liquorice Allsorts
Sieved apricot jam
Egg white

EQUIPMENT
No. 2 nozzle
Piping bag
Fine paintbrush
Pastry brush
Non-stick paper
25 × 18 cm/10 × 7 in
rectangular tin
18 cm/7 in round sandwich tin
30 cm/12 in round board

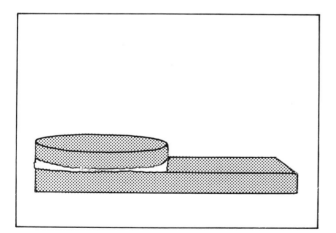

1 Bake an 8-egg sponge mixture in the round and rectangular tins. Trim the top of rectangle flat and trim the sides. Secure the round cake to one end of rectangle with butter icing.

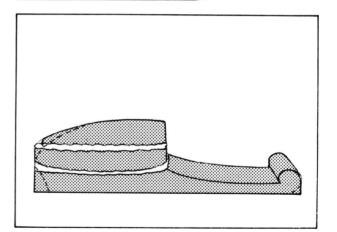

2 Cut out a section at the front of the sleigh as shown. Turn this piece over and place on top of the round sponge, sandwiching with butter icing. Trim the back of sponge layers to form a mound. Round the front end of sleigh and shape the back of sleigh as shown.

3 Brush mound with jam. Cover entirely with liquorice allsorts, layering in places, to form the shapes of the presents.

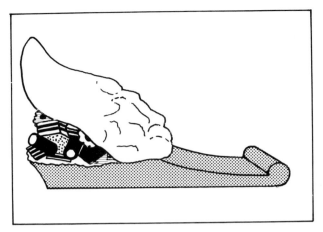

4 Roll 225 g/8 oz white fondant and, lifting with a rolling pin, ease gently over the presents, pressing lightly to reveal the shapes of the sweets.

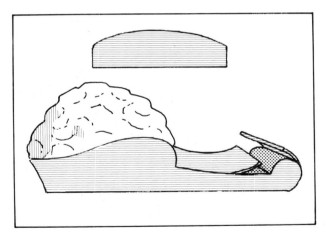

5 Colour 450 g/1 lb fondant dark green, using green and black colouring, roll out and cut inside, front, back and side panels for sleigh as shown. Leave to harden slightly. Brush sleigh with jam and place panels in position, placing inside section first, then front panel, back panel and finally sides.

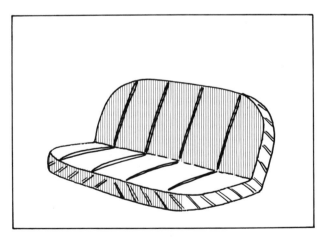

6 Colour 225 g/8 oz fondant yellow. Roll out about 12 mm/½ in thick and make seat from rounded rectangle as shown. Press the blunt side of a knife round edge and score lines across seat. Fold in half at a right angle. Brush base and back with egg white and place in position.

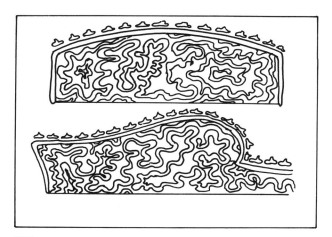

7 Colour 75 g/3 oz butter icing yellow and using no. 2 nozzle pipe decoration on side panels and front and back of sleigh as illustrated.

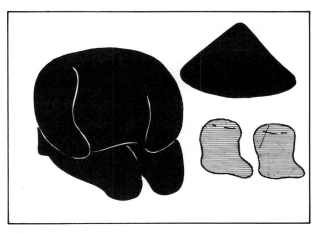

8 Model fondant Father Christmas as shown. Use small quantities of flesh for head, of brown for boots and belt and about 150 g/6 oz red fondant for body, arms, legs and hood. For hood cut a triangle from rolled fondant as illustrated. Join pieces with egg white leaving hood aside.

9 Place figure in position on seat. Paint blue dots for eyes. Secure hood in position tucking point in under the back of the head and bending sides round to fit under head at the front. Attach a tiny roll of white fondant for moustache and wider rolls to trim hood, cuffs and edge of coat. Use egg white to secure all pieces.

10 Using red, green, yellow and brown colouring and a fine brush paint paper patterns and ribbons on the presents.

Mother Pig with Piglets

INGREDIENTS
400 g/15 oz butter icing
50 g/2 oz marzipan per piglet
plus 50 g/2 oz
100 g/4 oz shredded coconut
Pink colour
Egg yellow con. colour
Chocolate drop

EQUIPMENT
No. 8 nozzle
Piping bag
23 × 18 cm/9 × 7 in
rectangular tin
28 cm/11 in round board
Candles

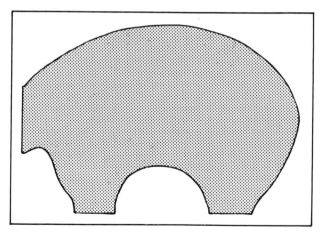

1 Bake a 6-egg sponge mixture in rectangular tin. Cut out shape for main body of pig as illustrated. Position on board slightly to one side.

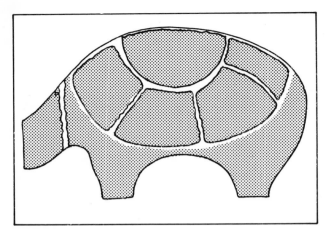

2 Use cut away pieces to build up body of pig to a rounded shape as shown, securing each piece with butter icing. Add piece on to snout to lengthen slightly. Colour 350 g/12 oz butter icing pale pink and cover pig entirely, smoothing surface.

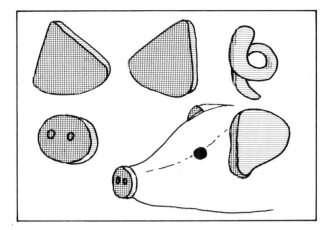

3 Colour marzipan deep pink. Roll 50 g/2 oz to about 6 mm/¼ in thick and cut out snout and ears as shown. Press out holes in snout with the end of a straw. Roll a tail. Press snout to cake. Attach ear, curving base edge as you do so and arching ear slightly before securing tip. Curl tail as you place in position. Place chocolate drop for eye.

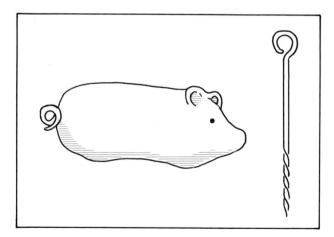

4 Make piglets from deep pink marzipan. Each piglet will take about 50 g/2 oz. Make rolls about 4-6 cm/1½ × 2½ in . Round one end and draw snout from the other with fingers and thumb. Pinch ears into shape. Using sharp point (e.g. a skewer) make 2 holes in snout and holes for eyes. Make a thin roll and attach a short curly tail. If for a birthday, the number of piglets can correspond to the age of the child.

5 Colour 50 g/2 oz butter icing and 100 g/4 oz shredded coconut yellow. Spread board with butter icing and sprinkle thickly with shredded coconut for straw. Place piglets along mother's tummy, some on top of others and one on the mother pig as in the photograph. Clear small circles in the coconut and using no. 8 nozzle pipe rosettes with remaining butter icing coloured deep pink. Place a candle in each.